A TREASURY OF DRIFTWOOD

and Dried Arrangements

"...some dried weeds, a piece of weathered wood,
a base or bowl...and the designer's eye"

A TREASURY OF DRIFTWOOD
and Dried Arrangements

by TATSUO ISHIMOTO

Crown Publishers, Inc. New York

For my wife, Kiyoto

Table of Contents

Foreword

Because in recent years foreign travel by Americans has accelerated, we are beginning to see a new sophistication in the way we live at home. In magazine photographs, in stores, and in our friends' homes we see the elegantly simple furniture of Scandinavia; shoji screens from Japan; colorful basketry from Italy, Mexico, and Hong Kong; and folk pottery from around the world.

And we see new forms of natural decoration being used in almost every room in the house, particularly dry arrangements of natural materials, displayed indoors in America as such materials have long been displayed in Japan.

This book is a treasury of such dry arrangements. Its purpose is to open a door for you to a rewarding hobby and an easily mastered decorative skill.

What is a dry arrangement?

Like flower arrangements, dry arrangements using driftwood are really "appreciations" of nature. Sometimes the appreciation is quite direct and literal: you recreate a natural effect, heightening that effect by your own efforts in cutting, placing, and rearranging. More often, the appreciation is not at all literal: the lines, color, and textures you work with are all from nature, but your final creation is original with you.

Unlike flower arrangements, dried arrangements are permanent, at least in the sense that they are nonperishable. An arrangement you like can stay in place indefinitely. Then, too, dried arrangements are quite independent of the seasons. You can use them in winter to display natural materials indoors, when your cut-flower garden is resting under a blanket of snow and perhaps when your budget urges you to pass by the corner florist.

In driftwood and dried arrangements you work with a very special color palette. All of the colors are nature's colors, but the brilliant flower colors are omitted. Mostly what you have are the earth colors—a range of soft grays and certain harsh grays; a long line of shades of yellow, tan, russet, and brown; a very few greens, and those mere gray-greens; almost never a pure white or black; never a primary color. With this soft and subtle color palette, form has a better chance because the colors will not intrude. The design is the thing; the colors can be lovely, but they are almost always subordinate.

Not many books* have been written about driftwood and dry arrangement, and there are no established schools, such as there are for flower arrangement. No one has laid down rules for others to accept, break, or modify; there is as yet little order and little controversy in this expanding, fascinating field of household decoration. But maybe it is just as well. Starting in, you are on your own. The basic design principles of Japanese flower arrangement are yours to follow if you wish. And often these design ideas prove helpful, particularly the development of the design in three levels and the use of asymmetrical balance. But just as often you can simply let your own eye, your own sense of design, and the nature of your materials be your guide.

Collecting your basic materials

Most driftwood arrangers I know sooner or later become driftwood collectors. Driftwood, of course, is a misnomer. I use the word only because there is no really accurate term for the kind of wood we are talking about. Driftwood can be beachwood, of course. You find it on ocean beaches, salt-washed, bleached, and weathered. Yet weathered wood occurs in so very many other places. The deserts of the American Southwest are perhaps the most rewarding sources of all. But riverbanks are marvelous sources, too, riverbanks in Missouri or Vermont or Georgia or anywhere. Moving water, rising and falling water, wind and sun, scouring gravel, all these

*One of the earliest in English, I think, is my own *The Art of Driftwood and Dried Arrangement*. New York: Crown Publishers, 1951, $2.95. A later, different one is my *The Art of Plant and Driftwood Arrangement*. New York: Crown Publishers, 1953, $2.95.

forces of nature create driftwood. Some of the finest pieces I've seen were collected a thousand miles from the nearest ocean shore.

When I look for driftwood, I pay attention not only to form but to surface texture, color, and size. I try to imagine each driftwood piece in use. Will it work best by itself, or is it most likely to contribute to a composition with dried materials? Can I improve it with a judicious saw cut?

Driftwood is not only handsome in itself; sometimes pieces have other possibilities. If you wish, you can make interesting and good-looking drawer pulls, book ends, lamp bases, even mobiles—using driftwood pieces. Large pieces can be placed in the garden or on your terrace, serving as natural and abstract garden sculpture.

Like all decorative features in your house, like any painting or tapestry or piece of sculpture, driftwood requires the right setting. You can use a fine driftwood piece all by itself—on a fireplace mantel, on a table, within a bookshelf, on the floor, fastened to a wall. But be careful. Like sculpture, the piece must be placed with great care. It will usually be happiest without companionship, with the stage all to itself.

There is also the matter of scale. A fine piece of driftwood shouldn't be cramped in its display place, nor should it be overwhelmed by the stage you give it.

For dried materials, walk the roadsides. Autumn is the best time to go searching. Annual weeds, their summer bolt shot, stand dry and stark, ready for your collector's eye to see their possibilities. For all collectors of driftwood and dry materials, country walking takes on a new, exciting dimension. So do slow drives on back country roads. Let someone else take the wheel. You can explore with your eyes and decide when to stop.

The three basic styles of dry arrangement

In this book I will not project any system or set philosophy. But there will be an arranged approach. I have been collecting driftwood pieces for more than twenty years, collecting dried materials, making and remaking arrangements using them, and over the years I have grouped my dried arrangements into three very broad categories. Let's discuss these for a moment. As you go through this book, arrangements in each of these categories or styles will occur again and again.

First, and most obvious, is *flower-arrangement* style. Here is a logical starting point for the experienced flower arranger who is using dried materials for the first time. These arrangements often look very much like flower arrangements, except that materials are dried and there is no water. Stems, typically, all start from one point in the container or base, and driftwood, if present, is usually not the center of attention.

Next is *landscape style*. Here is created a natural scene, the suggestion of some aspect of nature's forms on the land. Driftwood pieces become more important. Dried materials may spring up anywhere; they are trees or snags; they are stark natural forms on the skyline. The final arrangement will sometimes tell a story. A figurine may be part of the arrangement.

The third is *abstract style*. To me, these arrangements are the most difficult, the most challenging in every way, often the most fun. Your object is to create a three-dimensional abstract composition, your approach coming from the nature of the dried materials themselves. And each person viewing your result can read into it whatever he sees.

In abstract style you are on your own. Sometimes I call this "free" style because anything goes, as long as you are satisfied with the result. This approach corresponds in many ways to the very modern flower-arrangement styles now popular in Japan.

How to build an arrangement

In your design, establish three lines or levels—one tall, one medium, one low—all starting from a common point in the container or base.

Here is a rule of thumb to try out in establishing your three levels; tall, twice the length of the container plus its depth; medium, three-fourths of tall; low, one-half of medium. Flower arrangers use many such formulas; this one may help you get started.

I have a few general guide lines of my own. I always decide first where the arrangement is to go. This decision will affect all subsequent choices.

Next I choose my materials. As I study these, I let the nature of the materials themselves suggest the style to use.

I always start by placing the major pieces first—the most massive, or the tallest, or the most emphatic in form. Usually I work from the tallest down. My materials follow some general contour—triangle, oval, circle, or flowing curve.

Now and then I stand back and reconsider. If the materials suggest a fresh idea, I don't hesitate to change direction.

Your approach may differ. But let me urge upon you one general caution. Don't struggle too hard. A natural, spontaneous effect is what you are seeking. Nature is informal, and you are working with nature's materials.

Above all, be patient. Each driftwood piece requires leisurely study, and many compositions come together only by a slow process of trial and error, or trial and retrial.

How you want to work is up to you. If you have talent with a pencil, you may want to sketch your ideas first. I work standing up, but many arrangers I know prefer to work seated. Whichever way you come to prefer, the idea is to take it easy, take your time, and persevere until you know the arrangement is right.

Driftwood alone: The severe teakwood base contrasts with and sets off the driftwood's texture and twisted form.

Wood and weeds have decorative value

Dried arrangement: What does this landscape arrangement suggest to you? Weeds on a roadside? Or trees on a rocky skyline? This composition, in two levels, is somewhat unconventional.

Driftwood arrangement: The base is a shallow boat-shaped ceramic bowl. The arrangement, which is about fourteen inches tall, has three levels, driftwood dominating.

What are dried materials?

In this book you will see arrangements using weeds, grasses, plant stalks, and seed pods. Some plants I found already dried by nature; others I left out in the sun to weather and dry. The shapes resemble living plants, but they are much stiffer.

Treat them as you would flowers

Often your dried materials will resemble flowers in general form, as in this photograph. These are the plant forms to use in creating dried arrangements in "flower-arrangement" style. But you can achieve effects never possible with living plants.

Wind and weather often sculpture wood into marvelously twisted forms. This is a branch of manzanita weathered a silvery gray.

What is good driftwood?

Here are three pieces of driftwood I like, and there are many others elsewhere in this book. Your ideas may differ from mine, but the important thing is to search for pieces that suggest decorative ideas to you.

Left: This is a bit of sea sculpture found on a Pacific Ocean beach. Notice how the horizontal line of the base sets off the asymmetrical balance of the wood above. *Right:* Hand polishing was the method used to bring out the warm reddish color and fine grain in this piece of mountain manzanita, found in the Sierra foothills in California.

Magic-making: nature's drying out process...

Plants go through an astonishing change as growth stops, colors fade, succulence ends, stems stiffen, and leaves dry and wither.

What remains is a fascinating *essence* of nature. Here you have the bones of the plant world and a quiet memory of earlier lushness. Here are sculptural shapes and forms so intricate and beautiful, and at the same time so abstract, that doors open wide to the designer.

What other materials will you need?

Every arrangement needs a starting point. If you are an arranger of fresh flowers, your starting point must be a water container. If you work with driftwood and dried materials, you don't need the water or even the container.

Still, your arrangement must have a base. Your choice is wide indeed. Often I use a simple mat of masonite, cut to suitable size and shape and lacquered in black or gray or a color (often tangerine, grayed yellow, or off-white). There are many other possibilities: teakwood stands, low bonsai bowls (there are three sizes: 7″ x 10″ x 2½″, 8½″ x 5½″ x 2″, and 7″ x 4½″ x 1½″; bonsai bowls may be found in import shops or nurseries), bamboo mats, low but generous-sized ashtrays, and low porcelain or pottery dishes. The more bases you collect, the wider choice you will have each time you proceed with a new arrangement.

Many arrangers, myself included, couldn't get very far without a collection of stones. My own collection includes river-washed pebbles of various sizes and colors, broken volcanic and igneous rock, and pieces of shale and sedimentary shell-stone.

I use my stones in many ways. Sometimes they help support the arrangement and sometimes they simply conceal the needle holder, but they always add their bit to the total design. Usually their role in the design is subordinate, but not always. Sometimes I make a rock arrangement in which driftwood or dried materials are only an accent.

Figurines are a special, optional matter. I use them fairly often; some arrangers never use them. Figurines do help in landscape arrangements; they suggest scale and help the observer to read a story quality into the arrangement.

If figurines interest you, here are two suggestions. First, buy or find only those pieces that you consider handsome or charming. Second-rate figures will only downgrade your own efforts. Next, use your figures judiciously. Here is my own rule: always use small figurines in a large composition; large figurines with very little dry material. The idea is to never give equal importance to both.

What equipment will you need?

To someone used to arranging flowers, the making of driftwood and dried arrangements comes as a pleasant surprise. The stiff materials are easier to handle and everything is less floppy, more predictable. And every flower arranger will recognize the few pieces of equipment necessary: sharp shears, needle holders (and be sure to have some big, heavy ones), and clay.

A steady, secure arrangement should be your goal. Clay is a reliable adhesive; wads of it will fasten your holder firmly to the base. Sometimes you may want to use stones instead. The only problem is the obvious one: stones will be jiggly, so take care.

Learn to cut. Decide how high the tallest stalks in your arrangement will be, then cut to that height. But don't stop there; almost always, judicious further cutting will improve your material. As you know, different heights make for a more interesting composition, so trim your materials until you get the effect you want. Then put them in place, look at the result, and snip some more if necessary.

Above: Here are two incomplete arrangements. On the left, stalks are secured in a needle holder held down by clay. On the right, a stone weighs down the needle holder.

Below: Here are the same arrangements pictured above, but now complete. Desert curls conceal the holder on the left; rocks do the same for the arrangement on the right, and also complete the design.

A vertical driftwood arrangement, and,...

In this simple, well-balanced arrangement, the driftwood piece dominates and the dry materials play a secondary role.

After selecting a base in good proportion to the driftwood piece—in this case a polished plank—I set the wood in a vertical position. Then I used dry desert primrose to accentuate the curve of the wood, and bulkier materials (yucca pods, safflower, and stones) to broaden the base.

...step by step, how it was made

First I fastened the driftwood piece with clay, then braced it with stones. Next I stuck the primrose and safflower stems in another piece of clay, working to repeat the curved line of the driftwood. Finally, I moved the dry materials in close to the driftwood. Last came the yucca pods and stones *(see opposite page)*. The composition was complete.

Working in flower-arrangement style

An easy way to create attractive dry arrangements is to follow standard flower-arrangement techniques, using a flat container, a needle holder and clay. Dry materials, though arranged in a style similar to cut flowers, create a different effect. This graceful composition in flower-arrangement style uses three kinds of material in three levels.

In a bonsai bowl, first secure the needle holder, off-center, with clay, Place the tallest sprays first, then add secondary material in graduated lengths. Notice the height in relation to the width of the bowl.

How to build a landscape-style arrangement

When I make an arrangement that suggests a natural scene, I call it "landscape style." Dried plants can suggest trees; rocks will resemble cliffs.

On these two pages you see the steps in making a landscape-style arrangement. Don't worry about the holes in the bonsai container; your materials will cover them.

The starting point is the container, a driftwood piece in good proportion, and a few rocks. First secure the driftwood piece with clay and the rocks, then add the dry materials. These not only complete the arrangement, they conceal the clay. The finished arrangement reflects the shape of the driftwood.

This stand, because of its good proportion and simple design, heightens the beauty of this ancient piece of weathered wood.

Design possibilities with driftwood are endless

Driftwood occurs in an infinity of shapes, sizes, and textures, often beautiful but sometimes grotesque and disturbing. Your own eye will seek out the weathered wood with design potential. And each piece you find will need study. As you turn it around, its character will change, as will its color and texture and shadow pattern.

On these two pages you see five photographs of driftwood, all very different, but each with an interesting contour. It is difficult to believe all five are views of the same piece of driftwood. Notice how the characteristics of the wood change with each shift of position.

Experiment with each piece of driftwood in your own collection until you find its best position. Sometimes you will find a very promising piece that can be used at different times in different positions.

Desert driftwood with dry materials

This three-pronged piece of desert driftwood suggests a land-scape when used with dry materials. Giving the appearance of a windswept tree, it is secured to its masonite base by flat rocks that also contribute to the stark character of the landscape. The figurine of a deer gives the arrangement scale, and the stone at the base completes the landscape effect. Desert driftwood, typically, is warm in color and dried up in appearance, often rough.

Ocean driftwood suggests a
summer landscape

This three-pronged piece of ocean driftwood is similar in shape to the desert piece on the opposite page, but what a different landscape it suggests! By standing the wood upright in a flat container and adding delicate wild oat stalks cut to various heights, we get a summery, lighthearted result.

Ocean driftwood is usually gray in color and soft, with smooth surfaces.

Two tall arrangements: simplicity is the idea

The tall desert ribbon, in four vertically graduated lengths, contrasts with fan-shaped clusters of a lacy desert plant. Parrot's eye acacia is used as an accent at the center base, held up by dark pods that give strong color contrast and conceal the holder.

In this tall arrangement, the color transition from the dark pods at the base, through the medium tones at center, to the light colors at top, gives a feeling of growth. The base is a rectangular mat of masonite.

Two landscapes made with similar materials

Often the materials a flower arranger has at his fingertips suggest a theme for an arrangement. Dry tumbleweeds, torn apart into treelike shapes, are always useful in making miniature landscapes. Here, in a shallow container, are driftwood "logs," stones, dried vegetation, and the tumbleweed trees. The deer figurine adds interest and establishes scale.

Manzanita competes with the "trees"

Here I used almost identical materials to those in the last arrangement, with very different results. On a rectangular mat, a twisted piece of manzanita surrounded by tumbleweed makes an interesting silhouette. I planned this arrangement without a figurine, then added it later. The landscape was interesting without the little deer, but I liked it better this way.

How materials suggest the style of an arrangement

Sometimes an interesting piece of driftwood or an unusual dry branch will suggest an arrangement that is pleasing, even though quite unconventional.

That is what has happened here. The triangular twisted branch of driftwood suggested the idea of a mountain or canyon. When placed on a wide masonite mat, with stones added at the base for interest and weight, an abstract landscape effect was created. It needed a focal point to bring the elements together, so the figurine of a horse was introduced. What sort of landscape is it? What is it trying to suggest? This is for you to decide.

Dry arrangement with stones and figurines

Here is another unusual landscape built up on a flat base; unusual because this time stones are used alone, without dry materials. Figurines of horses are carefully placed among the stones to make a harmonious composition.

While this landscape certainly was not composed according to flower-arrangement principles, I have observed the Japanese rule of three in placing the stones: large, medium, and small.

Left: Here driftwood at the base serves to separate and emphasize the rhododendron foliage and blooms.

Right: The driftwood is the center of the composition. Bright pelargoniums flow around, below, and above.

You can use driftwood with cut flowers and greens

Many flower arrangers have discovered how driftwood can add character to their arrangements of fresh materials. I have been using driftwood in this way for many years, and I have seen many arrangements of this kind done by various masters in Japan.

If you place a driftwood piece vertically, make sure it is securely fastened before you build up the rest of the composition. Remember to use your modeling clay before you add water, because clay will not stick to wet materials.

Notice the three simple elements: vertical driftwood, a leaf arrangement in three levels, and a base of stones.

Compare the arrangement above. The elements are essentially the same, but the effect is quite different.

On a table: driftwood as abstract sculpture

Here an interesting piece of dry manzanita is displayed as abstract sculpture would be displayed on a living room table.

On a wall: driftwood as abstract sculpture

It is important to select the right size, texture, and shape for a particular setting. This driftwood piece, unusual in contour, hangs on a pine wall over a fireplace.

Why not experiment?

At right you see the result of an experiment. A few years ago I found an unusual piece of driftwood and decided to try to grow something on it. I soaked it in water, then planted two miniature conifers, to make a hilltop with trees. Pebbles in the container help assure good drainage when the plant is watered.

Another experiment

This time I planted a pine tree in a fern root from Hawaii. This type of fern root is often used as a growing medium for indoor plants. I wanted to give the appearance of a pine tree with a heavy trunk.

43

A tree on the skyline . . . or a forest

In this landscape arrangement, only three dried materials are used. Most important is the careful spacing of the "trees," which are poodle grass. The dark foliage of chorizantho-rigida provides balance and gives the feeling of a forest.

At right, a landscape with windblown "palms" was suggested by the curving branch of parrot's eye acacia. Rising from a needle holder on the flat container, it curves back over the base. Stones hold the acacia in place and complete the landscape effect.

Here is a study in textures...

Here desert ironwood is the dominant element. Its rough textural quality suggested the dry materials to go with it. The tall spray of parrot's eye acacia is the same one you saw on the preceding page. This is typical of dried materials; you can use it over and over again in different ways.

Rocks and small dry pods at the base add to a general feeling of heat and dryness.

. . . and here a study in contrasts

Here we have textures again, but the contrasts between them is what catches our eye. The perforated but otherwise smooth-surfaced vertical driftwood is in strong contrast with the spherical berries of the baby wood rose, and with the desert curls.

This arrangement suggests water, while the arrangement on the opposite page suggests dryness.

One driftwood piece with many aspects

You will often find driftwood with interesting contour and texture on more than one side. This is advantageous if the piece will be seen from all sides. If, however, it is to stand against a background, study it to see which side will be most effective.

Here are two arrangements with the same piece of driftwood. It is easy to create alternate effects by turning the driftwood and adding different secondary materials.

Left: Driftwood, rocks, jagged branches suggesting trees, and dry pods make up this simple landscape-style arrangement. *Right:* Figurines of horses, rocks, and wild oats create a very different design with the reverse side of the same piece of driftwood.

Dried miniature tree in a landscape arrangement

This simple but strong design is rather stark; it would go well in a modern room. The small tree rides in a black, boat-shaped container, anchored in rocks.

It is quite easy to find natural forms like these in the woods. If you use them with a harmonious base or container, you can achieve dramatic effects.

A landscape with unconventional materials

The landscape arrangement above shows how bold use of unconventional materials can create an original design. Egyptian corn, a cattle feed, might be considered unsuitable material by a flower arranger. But its tree-like forms make possible a charming landscape arrangement. The little horse gives the arrangement scale, and rocks and desert curls below anchor the trees and complete the scene.

The beauty of the arrangement on the opposite page comes chiefly from the texture of the piece of ironwood, hard and aged-looking. The ironwood is placed upright at the right and toward the back in the container (which was determined by the size of the driftwood piece), with pepper grass repeating the wood rhythms. The figure of a Chinese sage emphasizes the feeling of antiquity.

The round, low bowl partly conceals the rocks at the base of this arrangement. Your eye goes to the driftwood.

← A Christ's-thorn branch arranged to suggest a tree form. The rectangular container is ceramic. The driftwood suggests the earth from which the tree grows and also hides the needle holder.

Another experiment with dry materials

The exciting thing about dry materials is that you are free to try whatever the materials themselves suggest. You can make a landscape-style, a conventional, or an "abstract" arrangement, whichever suggests itself to your eye.

It took some daring to make the arrangement above. The strong curves of the Christ's-thorn and sal thistle, repeating the curved lines of the mat, were inherent in the materials. Vertical stalks of beetle weed balance the curves in this abstract arrangement.

A design in "flower-arrangement" style

This small and harmonious arrangement is visual proof
that dry materials used in a conventional arrangement can
be just as beautiful in line and rhythm as traditional living
flower materials. From a small, flat dish three sprays of
delicate wild radish rise from the center, with yucca tines,
cut to different lengths, curving inward from either side.
At the base, spherical teasel conceals the clay and holder
that support the arrangement.

Let the materials tell you what to do

Perhaps a tangle of desert curls and two curving primrose plants might seem unpromising material for an arrangement. But look again. Try fastening the light, twisted stalks of the primrose to a circular base, starting at the same point. Then use desert curls, stones, and one yucca pod to complete this interesting composition of curving lines. This is another instance in which the materials themselves suggested the theme of the composition.

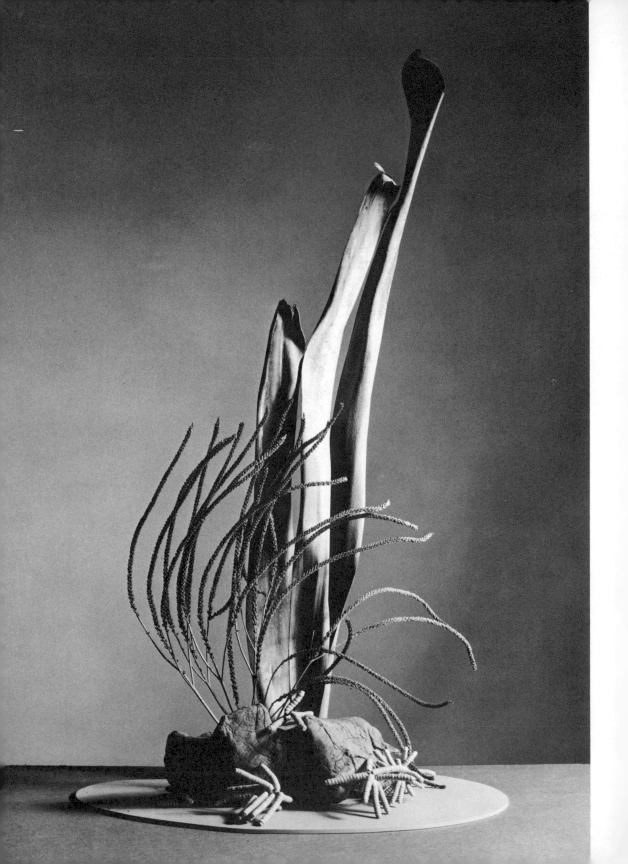

Single forms—in abstract and landscape styles

Here are two examples of single-unit arrangement. They are similar in basic structure, one expressed as a landscape arrangement (*above*) and the other as an abstract arrangement (*left*). A single and unusual tall form is dominant.

Left: Three tall desert ribbon stalks (one unit) curve upward from the center of a round mat. Curving rattails cross the vertical line; screw beans accent the foreground.

Above: Although the tall branch of primrose is similar in line to the desert ribbon, the stones on the base, together with chorizantho-rigida and pepper grass, give the feeling of a natural landscape.

Two quite experimental arrangements

For the arrangement above I chose a rectangular base, desert candles, desert curls, and pepper grass. The five candles were set at the left in back, and the desert curls swirled from right to left to achieve a unified effect.

Opposite: For this rather startling arrangement I chose a deep, long ceramic container. First, in back, I arranged some eighteen cattails of various lengths in a vertical pattern. Then I placed some strangely contorted pods among the tails until I achieved this quite fantastic pattern.

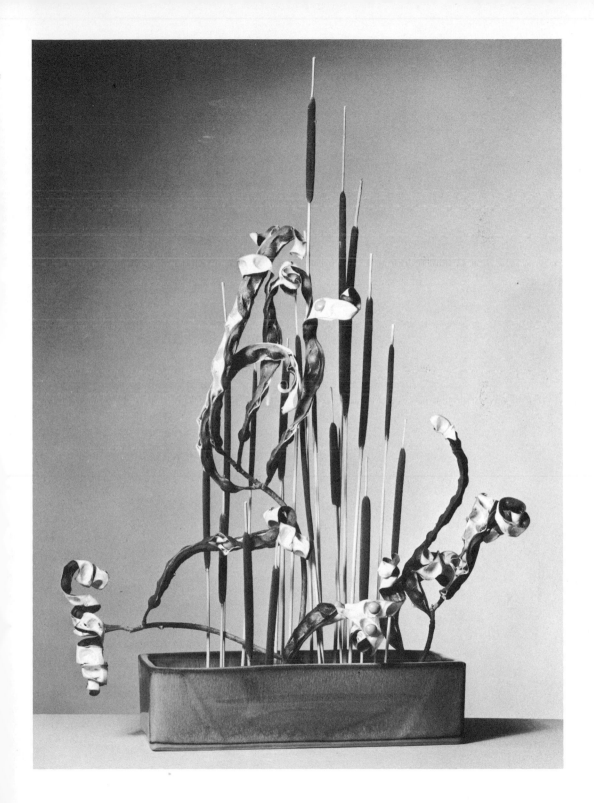

What is this? Maybe it's a desert lantern

Often you will find dry material of great interest, but puzzling in shape. The question is: how to use it? I call this composition, formed from a desert primrose plant, a desert lantern. I found it so fascinating I decided to place it on a Japanese teakwood stand with some spongy beach material as a cushion. The result was this unusual arrangement. Perhaps it might have been just as intriguing hung from the ceiling!

What is this? Your guess is correct

During years of travel I have seen many odd dry materials, but never until recently have I actually had my hands on this plant, which a friend brought me. Yes, it is cotton. To some it may be too familiar to seem interesting, but I found the cotton very effective as decoration, as in this simple arrangement. The Indian container is filled with sand to hold the cotton stems in place.

A miniature abstract arrangement

Here a small round bonsai bowl, only three and a half inches in diameter, was the starting point for a small abstract arrangement. The dry branches of dock you see were set in place first. Then, to give it a swirl and make things more interesting, desert curls were added at one side.

Sometimes a single form is enough

Sometimes you find an unusual dried form that does not seem to fit into any usual arrangement, or even to work well with other materials. Yet it is so interesting you want to display it. This desert primrose "lantern" becomes a conversation piece when placed to one side in a gravel-filled bonsai container. As the bonsai bowl has drainage holes, I covered them with cardboard and then covered the cardboard with gravel.

Experiment with strange materials

Don't be afraid to use strange forms to make unusual arrangements. When starting with the century plant in the arrangement above, the angularity of the branches seemed so dominant to me that I looked for some curving forms to soften it. By using a circular plate as a base and adding some pods, pepper grass, and stones, I finally achieved the result you see here.

This odd-looking driftwood suggested surrealist sculpture to me. I placed it on a dark rectangular mat and secured it with stones. I used rattails, curving from right to left, to soften the feeling of stress suggested by the wood.

Twisting, contorted Manzanita is the ghost wood

Manzanita takes fantastic shapes. This strangely contorted branch is such a piece. Originally it grew out of rock, with very little soil or moisture, and eventually it dried out in the form you see here. No wonder manzanita is sometimes called "ghost wood." Placed in a low, oval container with rocks and desert curls, it makes a striking arrangement.

66

Low-growing red manza-
nita, without leaves, suggests
some fantastic tree in this
landscape-style arrangement.
Rocks and dry materials on
the black mat at the base complete the scene.

This landscape ar-
rangement features a
dried cut branch of red
manzanita "tree," still
retaining a few leaves.
Rocks, driftwood, and
grass are arranged on
the free-form mat at the
base.

Driftwood sculpture... created by nature

Sometimes you will find a piece of driftwood sculpture so beautifully shaped by wind and weather that it can be displayed alone, as you would display any sculpture. All you need is a stand of just the right size and design to show off the driftwood to best advantage, and an appropriate display area somewhere in your house.

This manzanita is such a driftwood piece. The small picture (*right*) shows the same driftwood form seen from the opposite side of the stand, with the driftwood turned over.

Sometimes you can heighten nature's effects

Sometimes a piece of driftwood has rough places that can be gently smoothed. You can use sandpaper, following the natural grain of the wood.

Here are three views of the same beautiful piece of manzanita, smoothed by handwork to bring out its best qualities, then waxed to further improve the surfaces.

How to accent driftwood with dry materials

Above is a piece of hand-rubbed manzanita distinguished enough to be used by itself as a room decoration. Instead I placed it on a black mat and added a row of screw beans curving from right to left. The driftwood still dominates, but the dry material has made it a more interesting design, appropriate in a modern setting.

On the opposite page is another piece of twisted manzanita handsome enough to stand alone. However, by adding *dry* desert primrose and a piece of quartz to accent the line opposing its main diagonal, it becomes a different, and even more interesting, composition.

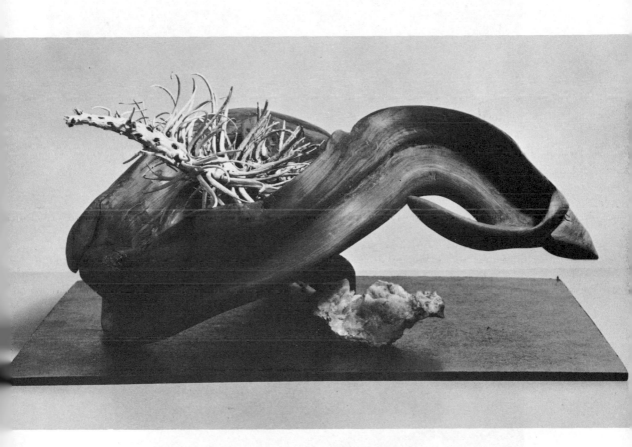

Even when a driftwood piece dominates your design, you usually will need secondary materials both to suggest a landscape and to complete the composition. This is the role of the three horses here.

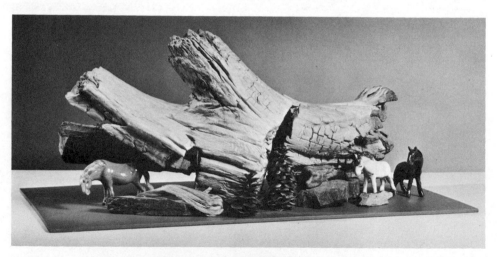

This is a similar arrangement, except that the driftwood piece is very different in character. Again I used three horses to complete the composition.

The figurine provides a focal point

The landscape arrangement above is complete in itself, graceful, and well balanced. The little deer, added last, provides a focal point. But the figurine was not absolutely necessary.

Sometimes I select a figurine *before* beginning an arrangement, planning the entire landscape in advance with the role of the figurine in mind. More often, I let the landscape itself dictate where to place a figurine, and what kind to use. To me, the sensible rule is small figurines in a large arrangement, large figurines with very little other material.

Sometimes there is more than meets the eye

The two landscape arrangements above are almost identical, but not quite. They do use the same materials in a similar way, but one includes a figurine of a Chinese sage—to suggest age. All the dry materials in these two arrangements were chosen because they looked "old."

The arrangement on the right has a contemporary feeling, perhaps because it uses natural materials in a geometric sort of way. I used three tall stalks of mullen cut to perpendicular columns of varying heights. At the base, horizontal slabs of driftwood, spherical teasel pods, and desert curls are all arranged in a formal, almost architectural order.

Dry landscape with the feeling of water

In their gardens the Japanese often suggest the presence of a stream, even though no water is used. In landscape arrangements, too, it is possible to suggest a waterside scene in a composition made entirely of dry materials. In the landscape arrangement at the left, see how the tall cattails (which always grow near water), stones, crooked driftwood, and waterbird figurine suggest the proximity of a stream or lake.

Above: This manzanita, like a tree twisted by ocean storms, seems to be growing out of the rocks, which resemble ocean cliffs. No water, but we think of the sea.

Just driftwood and rocks

It might not occur to you that driftwood and rocks, unsoftened by plant materials, can make a satisfying landscape-type arrangement. Here we see such an austere arrangement carefully built up in and above a rectangular container. The contour and grain of the wood are in enough contrast to the form of the rocks to make an interesting design.

Rocks and a single figurine

Here is another austere landscape-style arrangement, this time built of rocks alone, with a few sprays of foliage to suggest vegetation and a Chinese figurine placed in the focal spot. Notice how the rocky "cliffs" rise from the dark wood base, and how harmonious in scale are base, rocks, and figurine.

Assemble harmonious materials. The mat, bark driftwood, and horses all have curved forms. The flat rocks and sliver of driftwood are to be used for contrast. At right on the mat is a lump of clay.

Stand driftwood at the side of the mat and fasten into place with clay and one of the rocks. Insert dry stalks of dock into the lump of clay and move near the driftwood. Place the horses on the base in natural poses and add the other two rocks at the front.

How to build your design with dry materials

When you make an arrangement, the display area should determine the size and style of your design. So study the display space before you begin.

Above is the finished version of the arrangement started on the opposite page. First I selected driftwood suitable for the area where the finished arrangement would go. Then I chose secondary dry materials and the mat.

On the next two pages I will show some of the different results that are possible in arrangements built on the same principle, but with different materials.

Central motif: a twisted piece of driftwood, with rocks and thistles repeating its sharp points. Horses are used as part of the whole design, not featured individually.

This treelike driftwood is anchored by a needle holder. Large rocks suggesting cliffs are in front. Here horses stand out as important units that add interest to the scene.

Here is a way to make many landscapes

The critical thing about this landscape arrangement is the placement of the driftwood "tree." Note that it is far to one side on the mat, and that it curves over to the opposite side. It is thus necessary to balance the over-hanging branch by placing rocks in a mass below, with pepper grass and horses adding interest. The horses are placed to suggest the natural position of horses in a landscape.

This is a good formula to remember for making landscapes. Each one will be entirely different because of the different materials used. Compare this arrangement with the two on the opposite page.

Why not use underwater materials?

Beautiful forms and textures are found in sea flora and underwater materials, sometimes cast up on the beach. Shells, pebbles, and especially coral, lend themselves to making unusual arrangements. Consider the one above.

The idea of dried arrangements, as I see it, need have no set limits. Use the materials of nature, whatever stimulates your eye and hand, whether they come from riverbank, desert, seashore, or under the sea.

Why not a marine arrangement?

Often coral and shells are as delicate as flowers; you can easily build them into compositions, following the landscape-arrangement style. These are brittle materials, of course, so take care. As you combine the different fragile forms, incredible effects are possible. In the picture below, a flat base supports a variety of suggestive sea forms.

How to borrow a scene from nature

Here, tufts of moss clinging to driftwood branches suggest the foliage of a growing tree. To make this arrangement, I secured the branches at a point far to one side of the flat container, stones and clay holding the branch ends in place. Note how the branches curve back over the container to give a well-balanced look to the whole landscape. Note also that half the container is not used.

Working with curves and verticals

Here is a handsome, almost stylized arrangement. To make it, I combined pine branches, cattails, and pepper grass in a rather unusual way. Tall, spiky cattails form a rigid vertical grouping at the center, pine-branch ends curve across them from right to left, and pepper grass fills in at the base. The color contrast is quite startling: black container, black pine and brown cattails, white cattail stems, and the silvery pepper grass.

Are these windblown trees or dinosaurs?

The tall dry stalks of desert primrose curve and twist in a fascinating way. Here is a simple arrangement of four stalks on a round flat base, held in place with needle holder, clay, and driftwood. The success of the design is due entirely to the rhythmic curve of the plants.

This arrangement suggested windblown trees to me. I showed it to a friend, who commented, "Dinosaurs!"

What goes with driftwood? Monkey puzzle

An upright form of curving driftwood was firmly anchored
with clay on the center of my round mat. What to put with
it? In this arrangement I tried something unusual: I added
sprays of monkey-puzzle branch for a contrast in texture.
Dark pods at the base hide the clay and give a feeling of
movement and support.

Opposite page: A lofty single-unit arrangement with materials of contrasting texture. Observe the gentle curve to the left.

Above: Balanced arrangement of light, dry materials—delicate branches and sunburst thistles—with a curving driftwood piece at the base.

Right: Contrast in texture and shape makes a harmonious pattern in this arrangement of Mexican *chirohui,* yucca, and desert curls in a low container.

Arrangers' favorite:
the graceful desert trumpet

Among the many strange plants of the American desert, I particularly like the desert trumpet. How can you use this unusual plant in an arrangement? Like any other plant—combine it with related textures that will harmonize. Here you see the trumpets rising from a round mat, with camphor pods and stones to hold them, and a delicate petticoat plant fluttering above the base.

Opposite page: The beauty of this arrangement stems entirely from the strong rhythmic curve from right to left, rising from the stones that give weight to the design. Desert curls repeat the curved movement at the base.

In this delicate design, only two materials

Here branches of a smoke tree are set in a triangular container. Then thistles, stems cut from very tall to short, are placed in the center in graduated heights. The idea is to lead your eye from left to right, then up and back to the top left. This certainly breaks the flower arranger's rules, but the graceful result may justify the unorthodox method.

In this triangular design, many materials

The richness of texture and variety of design in this landscape arrangement are due partly to the many different materials and partly to the strong movement from left to right.

The tall, treelike elements are palm fronds and manzanita. Tumbleweed and yucca pods fill the central space, and rocks and pepper grass complete the landscape, with a deer on the center rock for you to discover as you study the arrangement.

Many ways to use the desert primrose

The dried stalks of desert primrose come in marvelously twisted shapes. Allow your imagination to suggest different ways to use them.

Above, left: Here desert primrose and safflowers are used together in a fan-shaped arrangement, with desert curls and driftwood below. The figurine is optional, but I like it there.

Above, right: Two desert primroses, one curve following the other, rise from the rear of a round container. Rocks and dry materials at the base complete the landscape, and if you look closely, there is a rabbit peering out.

Opposite: This tall arrangement is built up in flower-arrangement style. The desert curls and rocks below balance the tall stalks of desert primrose.

No one ever saw this before

The chance to create truly original designs is the great opportunity in dried arrangement. Your materials are unique, the combinations you make are your own choice, and the door to design is open wide. I don't think I have ever seen arrangements that closely resemble the two you see here. But this is only natural: no one else may ever have had this particular combination of materials before him.

Above: Delicate white branches are silhouetted against dark, upthrust driftwood, and white coral and pepper grass against dark rocks echo the contrast.

Left: Lantern-like stalks of the desert primrose rise above a bed of rock, whose harsh lines are softened by pepper grass. The curves suggest many things: a cello, a wineglass, a pear, a lamp chimney.

Here is a flower-arrangement style composition. There are the classic three levels, but the suggestion is a subtle one. Arrangements like this are easy to make with everyday roadside materials—dry stalks, pods, and leafless branch forms.

This tall, two-stem arrangement is a simple expression of contrast. The taller stem is bare most of its length; its companion is not. Below, the rocks and desert curls on the square base bring the composition into balance.

This arrangement, like the two on the opposite page, follows the flower-arrangement tradition. Here, the main point of interest is the opposition of the various curving forms. Note the repetition of curves— the stalk of the desert primrose, the desert curls, and the free-form mat on which the arrangement stands.

One design idea ... with different materials

Here are three arrangements, quite unlike in appearance and each made of quite different dry materials. Yet all three are built up in the same way. Compare the low, horizontal base lines established by container or mat, then consider the tall, central line made of several sprays rising from one

Slender lines go high, while broad leaves play the intermediate role; the base is a variety of clusters.

Compare this arrangement with the one at the left. The design is essentially the same, but this composition is simpler, stronger.

point at the back of each container. Next, note how the intermediate material links the tall line to the flat base, and last, see how the heaviest elements of all are massed at the base. In each arrangement your eye is led upward by a diagonal line, right to left or left to right. All three follow the same principle; the materials insure the variety.

Here are a dozen dry flower stalks rising above a twisted fragment of dry wood. In plan, this arrangement resembles the two opposite, but no one would ever confuse the three!

Starting with the container

Sometimes, when planning an arrangement, you may want to start with the container. Here my starting point was a low, rectangular pottery dish measuring 7 by 10 by 2½ inches. For about ten arrangements in this book, I have used similar bonsai containers, in three sizes. The other two sizes are 8½ by 5½ by 2 inches, and 7 by 4½ by 1½ inches. Bonsai bowls come from Japan; today many import shops and some nurseries stock them. Some are in mixed, glazed colors; others are unglazed, usually a dark brown. In this arrangement I filled the left side of the bowl with pebbles.

Container and materials must balance

Here is a different arrangement in the same bonsai container pictured at left. Both these arrangements, done in flower-arrangement style, follow a similar plan: high elements rise to the right. In this arrangement four stalks rise; in the opposite, only one. Notice the bonsai container; this is its opposite side.

Different effects . . . with the same materials

Your arrangements with driftwood and dried plant materials need not follow any set style. The materials themselves will encourage you to experiment.

On these two pages you see how identical pieces of yarrow can be used to create an utterly different feeling. *Left:* Cattails and yarrow, in flower-arrangement style, are set in an 8½- by 5½- by 2-inch container. *Above:* Used with driftwood, in landscape style, yarrow is cut low to give the effect of a ground cover.

A one-element arrangement

The photograph does not quite suggest how very small
this simple arrangement is. The container is 3½ by 1¾
inches. But small size or not, one basic requirement is met:
materials and container are in good proportion. This flower-
arrangement style composition is as simple as you could ask:
just one material, in asymmetrical balance.

An easy landscape arrangement

Here is a design useful for practice. The driftwood is almost exactly at the center, and the stones at the base, too, are almost exactly in balance. Only the dried plant material is off center. It is these that give the composition its variety and character.

A nandina branch, tall and curving

Sometimes you may wish to fill a space with a really tall arrangement. One answer is to combine an unusual assortment of materials. Compare the two photographs on this and the opposite page. Here the curve of the tall branch of nandina is repeated in the curves of the secondary materials. Again, I have filled the low bonsai container with pebbles.

112

The same nandina, but how different!

Here is the same nandina in a different bowl and in a very different composition. The flower holder is far to the left, and the yarrow and the eucalyptus pods do not echo the curve of the nandina, but instead stand apart from it.

You can use the same materials again and again

Used by themselves in the simple arrangement above, five delicate branches of dollar eucalyptus rise from an off-center holder in a bonsai container. At right, eight sprays of dollar eucalyptus leaves are set off by a cluster of dark eucalyptus pods below. You can find these leaves at many gift shops and florists; they work well in combination with many dried materials.

Do not be afraid to use your shears

Sometimes the very shape of your dried materials will suggest the arrangement you should make. But if the materials aren't that provocative, you may still be able to make them interesting by cutting. What you do is eliminate unwanted parts; you prune, trim, shorten, simplify.

Commercial materials usually come with stems the same length. The first thing to do is start snipping; you want stems of different lengths. *Left:* These agapanthus all were the length of the tallest until cut. *Above:* Here are the same materials cut still shorter to fit into a smaller arrangement with milkweed.

Two arrangements with wood roses

Many natural dry materials from far away are today very familiar to us. In Hawaii the wood rose is sometimes used in corsages. Here we like wood roses for dry arrangements. Above you see the graceful, curving wood roses in a dramatic container, presented by themselves in flower-arrangement style. At the left, the curving stems of baby wood roses rise from a needle holder at right in the container. The holder, held by clay, is neatly concealed by pods. The square container contrasts nicely with the curving forms above.

Where should the emphasis go?

The materials you select will often determine whether the emphasis should be above or below. In the landscape arrangement above, the lacy foliage of the "trees" overhangs the whole rectangular base and is the dominant element. A needle holder is actually the anchor in this composition; the stones that appear to be the anchor conceal the holder and suggest a rocky place from which the trees are growing.

The emphasis here is below

Contrast this arrangement with the one on the opposite page. The character of this driftwood and dry arrangement demanded a broad base with emphasis at the bottom. The tall, tapering desert cactus is softened by richly textured dry materials—petticoat plant, pods, and rocks—all resting on an oval black base.

Give your fancy full play

This arrangement suggested a sailboat to me, because of the shape of the container. I used yucca pods and desert curls like sails curving into the wind. All the dry materials are centered at one point in the container to give an ascending movement from left to right. An arrangement like this, without following traditional rules, can still be well balanced. No one else may interpret this as a sailboat, but the feeling of movement is unmistakable.

Secondary elements are important

When I considered this piece of driftwood it occurred to me that a small bear would look just right walking around behind the base. I selected a container the right size, added rocks for weight at the base, then a few dry materials. The driftwood is the main element, certainly, but it is the secondary materials that make this arrangement.

You are a stage designer, a dramatist

What dramatic compositions can result if you dare to do the unusual! Here you see a piece of tapering driftwood on a circular base, balanced only by rocks and weeds. Strong shadows highlight the scene.

Now that you have seen several dozen arrangements of driftwood and dried materials, and have studied my method of composing in flower-arrangement, landscape, and abstract styles, I hope you are ready to plunge in on your own. If you already are a flower arranger you should have no difficulty in beginning, and your first efforts should produce exciting results.

It has been my purpose in this new book to suggest the wide possibilities for making unusual decorative compositions with driftwood and dried materials. Do not be afraid to experiment—and let the marvelous natural materials themselves tell you how to proceed.